I0558010

SOMEONE

FINDS

ANSWERS

Published by Minds-Eye Manuscripts LLC, Grand Junction CO.

2nd edition. Copyright 2024. Content under AOC guidelines.

No copyright infringement is intended regarding drawings and pictures.

Introduction

Current human life should not be about satisfying our selfish needs. It should involve a breath of love for all of us. That and an understanding of reality and our potential can take us a good way to where it should be.

THOUGHTS ABOUT IT

Obviously, there is a problem in the world. Way too many of us believe that whatever we do as we live life along -when we do evil- will be washed away when we pass on.

That is, our stupidity, and "sins" following our lusts and selfish gatherings of things, will be forgiven by a spiritual creation, and we will reside there with the spirit in that space forever-a wonder land-happy with all resolved.

Alternately, some just do not give a darn.

The first fact countering this is that each of us is a member of a precious species, and harm to any of us works against the species survival, but more to sensitivity is that it damages the potential of our children's children to have a safe, happy, and productive life.

There is a way to solve the problem. Understand the reality of existence-our perception about the end of life and the consequences therein. Is it that all will be forgiven? No, there is a reality, an alternate pathway.

That is what the "Someone" in this book will discover. It may not reveal that "wishful" path but if you have half a brain - it tells you to make good choices on the way you live your life before you die (or stop) and help the children of our species have a future!

LEAD-IN

SOMEONE: He steps out of the house. On the sidewalk, he kicks a rock out of place and cusses aloud. "Darn, what a mess this business. The male in me wants sex although I have already made 2 kids, the body keeps giving problems, constipation, that damn scar on my leg itches, my eyes are getting weak, have a sore throat, and #*@## have I made some stupid choices, should have had those two years in the community school, would have had a better job, and now Sara is crying for divorce. I want to start all over, please, God!

Walks a bit to the park nearby, trips, falls flat face down! Lays there not wanting to get up, turning his head- there is a hand offered to help him up. On his feet looks at the helper, says thanks, and starts to move on. Helper says, are you Ok? Looks like you need help. He says, do not think anyone can. Helper says well sit a minute here on that bench. Do not want you to pass out on the way to where you are going. He does and he finds a friend!

Even though the friend looks like he is a thousand years old he enjoys their time each day, sharing thoughts, each with a cup of coffee.

Someone will never forget because on the sixth day on that bench with the Helper, he asks "Why do we even worry about all the crap we have created. Our souls are sure to either go to heaven or be reincarnated, you know the Hindu way. We should do just whatever the hell we want, take what we want, and enjoy while we can!"

The Friend says, "well you know it is pretty obvious that I have lived a long-long time, so if you want, I can share some knowledge on all that."

The old man then says "I have a bit of time each morning. Are you likely to be here regularly?"

"Yea, as I have been coming every morning to sit awhile, get away from all the B.S."

"Ok, see you here. Oh, and when we meet produce a question of something getting at you."

No promises, hope not to make you angry with me, but I will try to answer your questions with facts. And you can always go on the internet to check it all out!"

Q&A DAY 1

Telling of The Spirits

So, it begins the meetings of Someone and the Old Man. As it turns out each day addresses a question.

Morning, how are you getting along? Frankly, it was a hell of a night. Arguments, too many people wanting this and that, I am freaking exhausted! So, what do you want to know about, regards that?

Q: Providence will take care of me…right, you know help me out of this mess. Yes?

A: Well, that is a pretty good reach. People have wanted that since ancient times, a spirit helping them. But there have been millions and millions killed in religious-based wars, children essentially murdered. And this goes on to every disease, to every threat. Sorry, but that is not going to help you. Really. It is in the end up to you!

Q: Well, hell you are a freaking pessimist, oh well Anyway: When I die… my soul will be in heaven. Right! I can get away from all this mess there.

A: There are ideas about that…this already exists in many faiths, particularly those that hold a single "GOD." When one dies, they go to live with the creator in heaven. Be good according to the precepts of the faith and you will go there. In some of these be naughty (outside the precepts) and you go to a hell of a place. In all of these if you are a non-Believer," of our beliefs, watch out we may try to irradicate you. The interfaith wars are a significant part of human history and the suffering of millions of people.

Unfortunately, the ability to evaluate these in the light of what we know about space-time is quite limited because they are based on our "faith" to accept, from ancient stories handed down.

Most do have benevolence to others in some way in their original foundation. So, if you are a believer and do practice benevolence to ALL others you are Ok to live and die therein umbrellaed.

Also, it is worth pointing out that if there is a similar God, then that must be the same for all these faiths, so why kill each other. The precepts need redesign.

Even so, from ancient times there are those that suggest folks can be reincarnated. Now inside of this notion are ideas that would keep everyone being a good member of humanity. Further, our ever-growing knowledge of the reality of existence in space-time, allows this reincarnation idea to be examined. Would you like to dig into that?

Q: Hey that might be my way out of this mess! What is that all about"

A: Ok. I will give you a bit of an overview

Q: Wait, first do Christians believe in, reincarnation?

A: Birth, life, death cycle, or reincarnation… In Catholic churches, **one** in five parishioners believes in reincarnation. This does not mean that reincarnation or casting curses are approved by any Christian authority, but it does mean that they are popular among a very significant group of Christians.

Anyway, here is more of a fill-in. Reincarnation is a key belief within Hinduism. In Hinduism, all life goes through birth, life, death, and rebirth and this is known as the cycle of Samsara.

According to this belief, all living things have an **Atman**, which is a piece of Brahman, or a spirit or soul. And Hindus believe strongly there is reincarnation or afterlife. Most Hindus believe that all humans are in a cycle of death and rebirth.

When a person dies, their Atman is reborn in a different body. Some

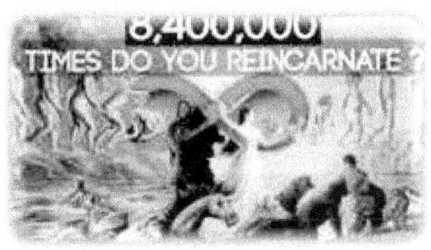 believe rebirth happens directly at death, others believe that an atman may exist in other realms.

In Hinduism, there is an outer limit of reincarnations. This is thought to be 8,400,000 Times.

In contrast to Hinduism Buddhism does not believe in reincarnation but in rebirth. The difference from Hindu ideology is that Buddhism does not believe that the soul is indestructible or eternal. There is nothing that goes through life, death, or rebirth.

Q: According to Hinduism, how does one know it they are reincarnated?

A: The concept is that Souls reincarnate many times and express that need because the cycle still is not complete, and it has not returned home.

Home may not be earth. If you feel in your bones that earth is not home and have other feelings of life on earth, such as wariness or tiredness, this could be a sign that you have been reincarnated.

You will ask, what happens to the soul when a person dies in Hinduism? The belief is that when someone dies, the soul is reborn within a different form. They believe that although the physical body dies, their soul remains and continues to recycle until it settles upon its true nature.

There are Some important questions regarding the Hindu premise. How do you attain a better life when you are reincarnated? How does Dharma (duties and laws) impact your next life?

Here is a fundamental proposition. Do good and you will be reborn to a better life, if you choose to do bad deeds, you will be born into a lesser life.

Q: I will bet there is an end to all that? What is the end of reincarnation called?

A: Moksha is the end of the death and rebirth cycle and is classed as the fourth and ultimate Artha (goal).

In short, reincarnation is defined as being reborn or the rebirth of the soul. When an old factory was converted into modern loft apartments, this is an example of reincarnation. When you die and then your soul comes back in a new body, this is an example of reincarnation.

This of course is like other religions-the soul goes to be with God.

Q: Sometimes, with all the stress and stuff I feel like I am going crazy. What would psychology say about reincarnation?

A: This would be "Transpersonal Psychology": Reincarnation, is literally "to be made flesh again", but it is a doctrine or mystical belief that some essential part of a living being (in some variations only human beings) survives death to be reborn in a new body.

Q: Ok, so is there any evidence of reincarnation happening?

A: Although those that hold the idea, will of course defend it in vigorous language. There was one trace of note. There have been reported that children can be found who themselves reported that they have memories of a previous life. More than 2,500 cases have been studied and their specifications have been published and preserved in the archives of the "Division of Perceptual Studies" at the University of Virginia (United States).

However, many of those children come from countries where most of the inhabitants believe in reincarnation. Just a few others come from countries with different cultures and religions that reject it. In many cases, the revelations (per se) of the children have been documented (their reports) and have corresponded to a particular individual, already dead. A good number of these children have marks and birth defects corresponding to wounds on the body of his previous personality. Many have behaviors related to their claims to their former life: phobias, philias, and attachments. Others recognize people and places of supposed previous life, and a few of their assertions have been made under conditions established by the psychologist.

Of course, the hypothesis of reincarnation is controversial. We can never say that it does not occur or will obtain conclusive evidence that it happens. The cases that have been described so far, isolated or combined, do not provide irrefutable proof of reincarnation, but they supply evidence that suggests some people 'feel" it is real.

R: You know what I am not wanting to come back as a worm! Reincarnation is not heaven! Can we talk about that I mean Heaven, tomorrow?

A: I am short on time then, but yes, see you then.

Q&A DAY 2

Light Finds Answers

Someone arrives and sits on the bench waiting for the old guy. His hair is all scrambled, not combed, shirt filthy. He looks a bit like a tramp and mumbles aloud despite the people walking along that can hear him. @#$#@ Boss! Then sighs relief as the old man sits down with two coffees and offers one to Someone.

Q: Hey thanks, and thanks for that info on reincarnation, but it says nothing about heaven, and you know I hope that is what is going to be my escape.

Q: But, well, I always wondered where is heaven? I mean it must be up there. What is up there…you know above the sky?

A: Well, "Space "is one term, the "Universe" is another but more appropriate to help in the most comprehensive understanding, the "Cosmos" and we are in it.

Q: Wait, I do not want a lot of gobbledygook talk, first how do we know about it?

A: Because of light. I will fill you in, but it does require some technical words. Are you good with that?

R: OK! (Oh… OK) … but go easy, please.

A: I will try! Let us begin back a step. "When stargazers go outside at night to look at the sky, they see the light from distant stars, planets, and galaxies. And light is crucial to astronomical discovery. Whether it is from stars or other bright objects, light is something astronomers use all the time. It provides them with confirmation. Human eyes "see" (technically, they "detect") visible light. That's one part of a larger spectrum of light called the "electromagnetic spectrum" or EMS, and *the extended-spectrum is what astronomers use to explore the cosmos.[1]* The EMS comprises the full range of wavelengths and frequencies of light that exist: radio waves, microwave, infrared, visual (optical), ultraviolet, x-rays, and gamma rays.

The part we humans see is a very tiny sliver of the wide spectrum of light that is given off (radiated and reflected) by objects in space and on our planet. For example, the light from the Moon is light from the Sun that is reflected off it.

Did you know, Human bodies also emit (radiate) infrared (sometimes referred to as heat radiation). If people could see in the infrared, things would look very different.

R: Oh yes, I have seen pictures of those IR things soldiers use to see the enemy.

A: Right, that is an example. And, other wavelengths and frequencies, such as x-rays, are also emitted and reflected. X-rays can pass through objects to illuminate bones. Ultraviolet light, which is also invisible to humans, is quite energetic and is responsible for sunburned skin.

1. **The old man is reviewing his knowledge gained in an article** by Collins Petersen on July 03, 2019.

Anyway, as you may know, regards the Cosmos (particularly or part of it the Universe) Astronomers measure many properties of light, such as luminosity (brightness), intensity, frequency or wavelength, and polarization. *Each wavelength and frequency of light lets astronomers study objects in the universe in different ways.*

The speed of light -an awesome 299,729,458 meters a second is also an important tool in determining distance. For example, the Sun and Jupiter (and many other objects in the universe) are natural emitters of radio frequencies. Radio astronomers look at those emissions and learn about the objects' temperatures, velocities, pressures, and magnetic fields.

One field of radio astronomy is focused on searching out life in other worlds by finding any signals they may send. *That is called the search for extraterrestrial intelligence* (SETI).

Astronomy researchers are often interested in the luminosity of an object, which is the measure of how much energy it puts out in the form of electromagnetic radiation. *That tells them something about activity in and around the object.*

In addition, light can be "scattered" off an object's surface. *The scattered light has properties that tell planetary scientists what materials make up that surface.* For example, they might see the scattered light that reveals the presence of minerals in the rocks of the Martian surface, in the crust of an asteroid, or on Earth.

Infrared light is given off by warm objects such things as protostars (stars about to be born), planets, moons, and brown dwarf objects. When astronomers aim an infrared detector at a cloud of gas and dust, for example, the infrared light from the proto-stellar objects inside the cloud can pass through the gas and dust. *That gives astronomers a look inside the stellar nursery.* Infrared astronomy discovers young stars and seeks out worlds not visible in optical wavelengths, including asteroids in our own solar system. *It even gives them a peek at places like the center of our galaxy, hidden behind a thick cloud of gas and dust.*

As said, Optical (visible) light is how humans see the universe; we see stars, planets, comets, nebulae, and galaxies, but only in that narrow range of wavelengths that our eyes can detect. It is the light we evolved to "see" with our eyes.

Interestingly, some creatures on Earth can also see into the infrared and ultraviolet, and others can sense (but not see) magnetic fields and sounds that we cannot directly sense. We are all familiar with dogs who can hear sounds that humans cannot hear.

Ultraviolet light is given off by energetic processes and objects in the universe. An object must be at a certain temperature to emit this form of light. Temperature is related to high-energy events, and so we look for x-ray emissions from such objects and events as newly forming stars, which are quite energetic. Their ultraviolet light can tear apart molecules of gas (in a process called photodissociation), which is why we often see newborn stars "eating away" at their birth clouds.

And this opportunity for knowing what is up there has more input!

X-rays are emitted by even more energetic processes and objects, such as jets of superheated material streaming away from black holes.

Supernova explosions also give off x-rays. Our Sun emits tremendous streams of x-rays whenever it belches up a solar flare.

Gamma-rays are given off by the most energetic objects and events in the universe. Quasars and hypernova explosions are two good examples of gamma-ray emitters, along with the famous "gamma-ray bursts".

And the bottom line is that Detecting Various Forms of Light confirms the existence of space and that it holds stars, planets, and much more.

Astronomers have different types of detectors to study each of these forms of light. The best ones are in orbit around our planet, away from the atmosphere (which affects light as it passes through).

There are some very good optical and infrared observatories on Earth (called ground-based observatories), and they are located at very high altitudes to avoid most of the atmospheric effects. The detectors "see" the light coming in. The light might be sent to a spectrograph, which is a very sensitive instrument that breaks the incoming light into its component wavelengths. It produces "spectra", graphs that astronomers use to understand the chemical properties of the object. For example, a spectrum of the Sun shows black lines in various places; those lines indicate the chemical elements that exist in the Sun.

Incidentally, light is used not just in astronomy but in a wide range of sciences, including the medical profession, for discovery and diagnosis, chemistry, geology, physics, and engineering. It is really one of the most important tools that scientists have in their arsenal of ways they study the cosmos.

A: So, how am I doing, if too much info, I will stop.

R: No, no not at all and the coffee is keeping me from falling asleep.

A: Great, I will try to wrap up though. **Into this also comes the question of time**. Because as we look up into the cosmos or as you would say, "The heavens," we find that we must deal with it.

Of course, Everyone experiences time-every day- but a rigorous and comprehensive understanding of the topic is lacking for most of us. However, knowing about the Cosmos is very important.

We do know some things, especially when we look at time through the lens of that which is called <u>Special</u> and <u>General Relativity</u>. Einstein's work taught us many things: that space and time are connected, that you can never travel faster than light, that our universe has a finite (limited) age, and that different observers experience different lengths of time[1]. So, we have learned that where our earth is, i.e., in our universe it is 13.77 billion years old, according to our current best estimates, which are very good, thank you very much!

But when special relativity is invoked, we also understand that everyone measures time differently, depending on their speed. We, on Earth, whizzing around the sun, with the sun spinning around the Milky Way, and the Milky Way blasting through the intergalactic vacuum should have

~~~~~~~~~~~

Note: In this discussion the old man is using information by **Paul Sutter**, published March 16, 2019.

a different perspective on the flow of time than someone else on a different planet around a different sun in a different galaxy. That said, how can we pin down a "real" age of the universe?

Here is the trick. Yes, according to special relativity, different observers have different measures of time.

But our whole entire universe is not fully described by special relativity. The tools that we use to understand matters cosmologically are provided by its bigger brother, general relativity. And when we look at the history of the universe from general relativity's viewpoint, we find that the cosmos … well, has a history.

This leads to a very important point as to what is in the Cosmos. We are **in a universe and it expands with time**!

It was smaller in the past, and it will be bigger in the future. There is a direct connection between a particular moment in time and a particular size of the universe.

This is what allowed scientists to construct what amounts to a universal clock, a timepiece that has been ticking away for over 13 billion years!

Yes, the motion of Earth through the universe changes that clock slightly, but with the tools of general relativity, we can subtract that out and work out the "real" age of our universe which is better than 13 billion years old.

R: Ok, that last bit loses me, but I know about Einstein, so I am sitting here after 13 billion years to me. Right!

A: Right-that is the rational conclusion.!

Well, let that be a start… I must go. Want more in a.m. That is, in our human time?

R: Someone says yes! OK, old man, but I still do not know-I mean you have not told me where heaven is!

Q&A DAY 3

What Is It Up There?

It is a beautiful day. The sky is clear, and you can look deep into the blue. Someone is sitting on the bench before the man comes.

He, as usual, is looking sad and dejected. Soon the "Old Man" comes along and brings with him some photos.

Someone comments I do not want to look at family pics, I just what an answer!

Q: Where is heaven? I know it is up there!

A: Well, let us first start by correct referencing.

We will be talking about the "Universe," that is, our most immediate reference in the Cosmos in Intergalactic Space.

The "Universe," to paraphrase the British biologist JBS Haldane, "is not stranger than we imagine. It is so vast that it defies imagination."

That language is saying "imagining" is not the way to deal with it, we use facts!

Let me amplify. Here are nine of the most astounding space discoveries of recent times.

1. The Universe was born

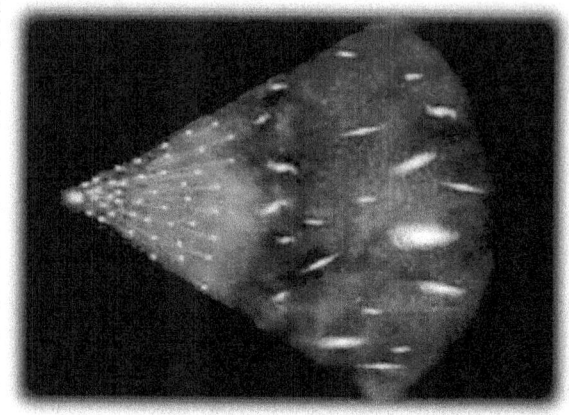

What we believe is our Universe has not existed forever. It was born. 13.82 billion years ago. all matter, energy, space, yes, and even time – erupted into being in a titanic fireball called the "Big Bang." And many galaxies formed!

The explosive fireball began expanding out of the cooling debris, and there eventually congealed the galaxies–great islands of stars of which our Milky Way is one galaxy among an estimated two trillion. This, in a nutshell, is the Big Bang theory.

Whatever way you look at it, the idea that the Universe popped into existence–that there was a day without a yesterday– is utterly bonkers. But that is what the evidence tells us.

An immediate question arises: what happened before the Big Bang? There are some explanations that I will get to later.

Now we are considering what is up there to get to the point of what the Cosmos does.

~~~~~~~~~

(The photo is a representation of the birth and growth of the Universe. Credit: BSIP SA / Alamy Stock Photo)

2. There is a supermassive black hole at the heart of every galaxy

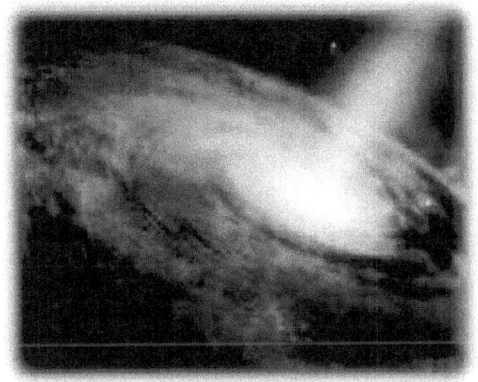

Active galaxies often pump out 100 times lighter than a normal galaxy. With the discovery in 1963 of quasars, it was clear that light comes not from stars but from a central region smaller than the Solar System.

The only conceivable energy source is matter heated to incandescence as its swirls down onto a giant black hole up to 50 billion times the mass of the Sun.

In the 1990s, NASA's Hubble Space Telescope found that, although active galaxies account for only about 1% of galaxies, supermassive black holes are no anomaly.

Almost every galaxy, including our Milky Way, contains one, but starved of a food supply, most have switched off.

What are supermassive black holes doing in the hearts of galaxies? They can be the seeds around which galaxies congealed. Or they may be spawning newborn galaxies. These are being further investigated in astrophysics. But they are there and that tells us of the awesome power in the Universe. More than that they offer the potential for universes to soak into the realm of a greater existence, within the Cosmos.

~~~~~~~~~~

Galaxies are illuminated by the black holes at their centers. Credit: Claudio Ventrella / Getty Images

3. The Universe has the same temperature everywhere.

The Old Man holding a photograph then points to the colored areas and says, "This is a snapshot of the "Cosmic--Microwave Background".

That is the heat left over from the Big Bang when the Universe was just 380,000 years old, as seen by the Planck Telescope. It shows tiny temperature fluctuations that correspond to regions of different densities: the seeds that would grow into the stars and galaxies of today.[1]

The heat of the Big Bang fireball was bottled up in the Universe. It had nowhere to go, so it is still around us today.

The weird thing is that its temperature – 2.725°C above absolute zero or – 270°C, the lowest temperature possible is the same everywhere.

1. Credit: ESA and the Planck Collaboration

Yet, if we imagine cosmic expansion running backward, like a movie in reverse, we find that parts of the Universe that are on opposite sides of the sky today were not in contact when the fireball of radiation broke free of matter.

In other words, there has been insufficient time for heat to travel between them and the temperature to equalize since the Universe's birth.

Astronomers fix this by maintaining that early on, the Universe was much smaller than expected, so heat got around easily. To get from this smaller size to its present size, the Universe had to go through an initial burst of superfast expansion, known as Inflation.

4. 95% of the Universe is invisible

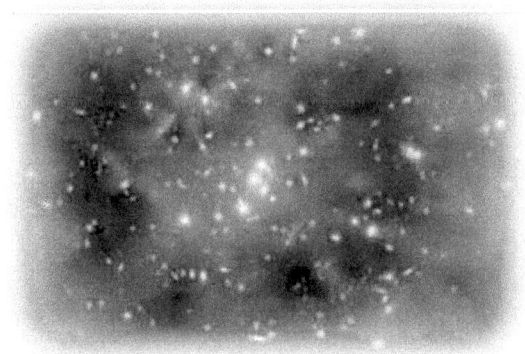

The dark ring superimposed on this Hubble image is a representation of the **dark matter** thought to be causing the distortions in the galaxy cluster.

Credit: NASA, ESA, and M.J. Jee (Johns Hopkins University).

There is a discovery so amazing that it has yet to trickle into the consciousness of most working scientists: everything science has been studying these past 350 years is but a minor contaminant of the Universe. That is, only about 4.9% of the mass-energy of the Universe is atoms: the kind of stuff you, me, the stars, and galaxies are made of (and, of that, only half has been spotted with telescopes).

About 26.8% of cosmic mass energy is invisible dark matter, revealed because it tugs with its gravity on the visible stuff.

Candidates for what makes up dark matter include hitherto unknown subatomic particles and black holes made in the Big Bang.

But, in addition to dark matter, there is dark energy, accounting for 68.3% of the mass energy of the Universe. It is invisible, fills all of space, and is accelerating with cosmic expansion. The best theory, which is – quantum theory – overestimates its energy density by a factor of one followed by 120 zeroes!

Many notions can be taken away from this. But clearly, we are such a small bit in this that we may not be as "cosmologically relevant" as we think.

5. Most of the stuff in the Universe has repulsive gravity.

The Universe is expanding, its constituent galaxies flying apart like pieces of cosmic shrapnel in the aftermath of the Big Bang. The only force operating should be gravity, which acts as a web of elastic between the galaxies, slowing them down.

But in 1998, contrary to all expectations, astronomers found that the expansion of the Universe is speeding up!

To explain it, they postulated the existence of invisible stuff, which as noted above, they have termed dark energy, which fills space and has repulsive gravity.

It is the repulsive gravity of this dark energy that is accelerating cosmic expansion!

Dark energy accounts for almost two-thirds of the mass energy of the Universe. School science is therefore behind the times in saying that gravity sucks. In most of the Universe, it blows!

6. The Sun is producing only a third of the neutrinos expected

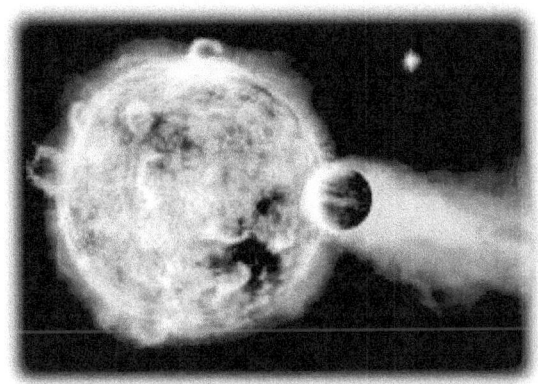

The old man hands Someone this picture. It is a depiction of our Sun (sun alone captured by NASA's Solar Dynamics Observatory).

Hold up your thumb. 100 billion neutrinos are passing through your thumbnail every second. 8.5 minutes past they were in the heart of the Sun (neutrino cloud depicted).

Solar neutrinos are a by-product of sunlight-generating nuclear reactions. When Ray Davis set out to detect them with 100,000 gallons of cleaning fluid down a mine in South Dakota, he expected to confirm the standard picture of the Sun.

Instead, he found only a third of the expected neutrinos, something that was not only confirmed by later experiments but led to his Nobel Prize.

Neutrinos are ghostly subatomic particles existing in a weird quantum superposition – akin to an animal that is simultaneously a cow, a pig, and a chicken.

As they travel from the Sun, they flip between being an electron neutrino, a muon neutrino, and a tau neutrino, which is why experiments sensitive to only one type pick up a third of the expected number.

R: So, what, what does that have to do with what is up there.

A: It relates that Galaxies can be quite different than the usual expectations of just some places with planets. So much of our Universe has properties of total power and awesomeness! And this follows what I describe next.

7. Most planetary systems are different from ours!

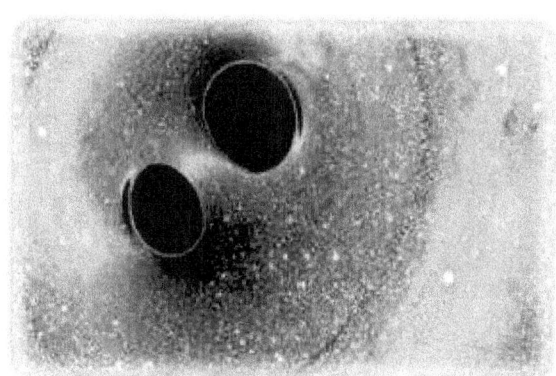

Here is an artist's conception of a so-called hot Jupiter*. These gas giants orbit close to their star and are common in other systems, but not in our own Solar System.

However, Scientists hate to invoke anything special about our situation in the Universe. 'Special' is improbable while 'typical' is probable.

But the discovery of planets around other stars – at last count, more than 3,500 have been confirmed – has created a headache. As far as we know today, none is like our own!

There are super-compact planetary systems in which all planets orbit closer to their parent star than Mercury, the innermost planet of the Solar System does to the Sun. There are Jupiter-mass planets that must have migrated inward. There are planets in highly elliptical orbits, like those of comets. And some planets orbit the wrong way around their stars.

Given that planets are believed to congeal from gas and dust swirling in

* Credit: NASA/Ames/JPL-Caltech

the same direction around a newborn sun this latter discovery is especially hard to explain.

You see, yet nobody knows whether the unusualness of our Solar System has anything to do with humans, but though infinitely small we obviously are unique.

8. The first gravitational waves detected came from a binary black hole system nobody predicted,

On 14 September 2015, gravitational waves were detected on Earth for the first time.

These ripples in the fabric of spacetime predicted by Einstein in 1916 – came from the merger of two black holes in a distant galaxy.

Briefly, the power pumped out was 50 times greater than that of all the stars in the Universe combined. But this was not the only jaw-dropping aspect of the event.

Each of the black holes was in the 30 solar mass range. Since a black hole is what is left after most of a star has blown into space as a supernova, the precursor stars must have weighed at least 300 solar masses.

Such stars are incredibly rare today.

But the two black holes could have been remnants of the very first generation of stars – thought to be huge – or even primordial black holes, born in the inferno of the Big Bang itself.

9. We appear to be alone!

This is a picture of the antennas of the Atacama Large Millimeter and submillimeter Array (ALMA) in the Chilean Ande (Credit: ESO/C.)

Observing in this way it is evident that 100,000,000,000,000,000,000,000 stars are in the Universe. And there are more planets than stars! Yet in all this immensity there is only one place we know of where life exists: Earth!

Despite searches for intelligent signals, no sign of intelligent extraterrestrial life has been found. In fact, there is a good argument that if such life-forms exist out there, not only should we see signs of them, but they should already have come here.

"Where are they?" the physicist Enrico Fermi famously asked. Some astronomers think the answer is we are alone, that we must be the first.

But the absence of evidence is not evidence of absence. It took three billion years for us to go from single cells to complex life, which suggests taking this step is hard.

Technological civilizations' 1like ours may be rare and their lifetimes short; we may have missed any others by millions or billions of years. The other alternative is that the nearest one may simply be too far away for us to detect.

R: Oh, I see what you are telling me.

We have come about, one of billions upon billions of unique explosions in the massive explosive power in the chemistry of our Universe. Right?

A: That is close, but there is more to consider. I will come here tomorrow to go on if you want.

R: Ok, but I must leave after an hour…seeing a divorce lawyer. I am thinking our Universe (Galaxy) results from random reactions from countless chemicals in a unique spontaneous reaction vessel.

And the time they are talking and looking at pictures does bring the two closes to Someone's time to go to work, so they shake hands, while the photos are handed over to Someone and they agree to meet the next day.[1]

1.Marcus Chown is a science writer and author. This information originally appeared in the January 2018 issue of BBC Sky at Night Magazine.

Q&A DAY 4

Filling in the Vast Cosmos

Both Someone and the Old Man arrived at the bench at the same time, but it was the old man to bring the coffee, which had become a habit.

They sat down stretched legs and looked at each other in respect (growing friendship) the discussion began.

Q: Well Old Friend: Like said---I have a challenge (the divorce decree) and must leave in no more than an hour. I am still trying to find an answer, as to where God is, certainly must be up there somewhere. Oh, if not that Outside of that. Our universe.

A: Actually, there is more. But first I am sorry you are going through what you are. I do believe that time will help heal those wounds.

To the subject though. Based on the rate of cosmic expansion, astrophysicists estimate that the "observable" universe is **a sphere measuring about 93 billion light-years across**. However, beyond that, the Universe extends much farther.

That is, it is expanding way beyond our ability to see. We are a new "Observationalist."

Humans began the physical exploration of space just during the 20th century with the advent of high-altitude balloon flights. This was followed by crewed rocket flights and, then, crewed Earth orbit, first achieved by Yuri Gagarin of the Soviet Union in 1961.

Due to the high cost of getting into space, human spaceflight has been limited to low Earth orbit and the Moon.

On the other hand, uncrewed spacecraft have reached all of the known planets in the Solar System, so our knowledge has become most impressive.

As we proceed with getting descriptions and definitions straight it is important to understand. "Outer Space", commonly shortened to **Space"**, in most reported jargon, relates to just the expanse that exists beyond Earth and its atmosphere and between celestial bodies.

However, it is clear, that there is more than our galaxy, even that outer

space is not completely empty—it is in fact a hard-vacuum containing a low density of particles, predominantly a plasma of hydrogen and helium, electromagnetic radiation, magnetic fields, neutrinos, dust, and cosmic rays.

The plasma between galaxies is thought to account for about half of the baryonic (ordinary) matter in the universe, having a number density of less than one hydrogen atom per cubic meter (and a temperature of degrees(Kelvin).

Local concentrations of matter have condensed into stars and galaxies.

However as already noted studies indicate that 90% of the mass in most galaxies is in an unknown form, usually called dark matter, which interacts with other matter through gravitational but not electromagnetic forces.

Note: The Old man is answering Someone in this section using an information document in Wikipedia https://en.wikipedia.org/wiki/Outer_space#cite_note-CBE2008-1

And, observations suggest that the majority of the mass-energy in the observable universe is *dark energy*, a type of vacuum energy that is poorly understood. (Remember I promised to get back to this)

R: Hmm, yes that last and dark space you have brought up before. That is very interesting can you tell me more!

A: Absolutely, I will first tell more of the "Filling" and what leads to the "Dark."

Intergalactic Space takes up most of the volume of the universe, but even galaxies and star systems consist almost entirely of empty space.

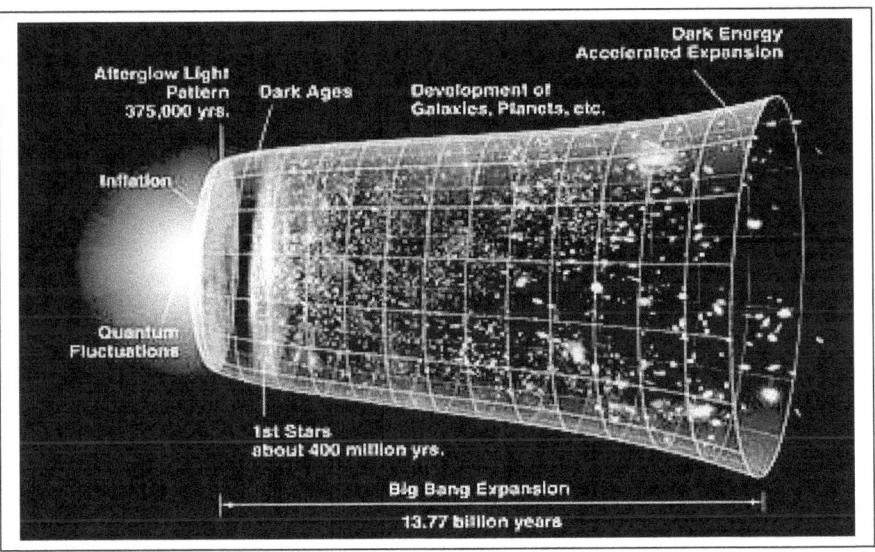

.The depiction is an artist's concept of the metric expansion of space, where a volume of the Universe is represented at each time interval by the circular sections. At left is depicted the rapid inflation from the initial state, followed thereafter by steadier expansion to the present day, shown at right. The size of the whole universe is unknown. Some propose it is likely "infinite" in extent. Because of its explosive origin (Big Bang), it clearly came from outside of its expanded self.

According to the Big Bang theory, the very early Universe was an

extremely hot and dense state about 13.8 billion years ago which rapidly expanded. About 380,000 years later the Universe had cooled sufficiently to allow protons and electrons to combine and form hydrogen—the so-called recombination epoch.

When this happened, matter and energy became decoupled, allowing photons to travel freely through the continually expanding space. The matter that remained following the initial expansion has since undergone gravitational collapse to create stars, galaxies, and other astronomical objects, leaving behind a deep vacuum that forms what is now called "outer space". As light has a finite velocity, this theory also constrains the size of the directly observable universe.

The present-day shape of the universe has been determined from measurements of the cosmic microwave background using satellites like the Wilkinson Microwave Anisotropy Probe. These observations indicate that the spatial geometry of the observable universe may be "flat", meaning that photons on parallel paths at one point remain parallel as they travel through space to the limit of the observable universe, except for local gravity. Outer space is the closest known approximation to a perfect vacuum. It has effectively no friction, allowing stars, planets, and moons to move freely along their ideal orbits, following the initial formation stage.

However, the deep vacuum of intergalactic space is not devoid of matter, as it contains a few hydrogen atoms per cubic meter. By comparison, the air humans breathe contains about 10^{25} molecules per cubic meter. The low density of matter in outer space means that electromagnetic radiation can travel great distances without being scattered: the mean free path of a photon in intergalactic space is about 10^{23} km or 10 billion light-years. Despite this, extinction, which is the absorption and scattering of photons by dust and gas, is an important factor in galactic and intergalactic astronomy.

Stars, planets, and moons retain their atmospheres by gravitational attraction. Atmospheres have no clearly delineated upper boundary: the density of atmospheric gas gradually decreases with distance from the object until it becomes indistinguishable from outer space. The Earth's atmospheric pressure drops to about 0.032 Pa at 100 kilometers (62 miles) of altitude, compared to 100,000 Pa for the International Union of Pure and Applied Chemistry (IUPAC) definition of standard pressure. Above this altitude, isotropic gas pressure rapidly becomes insignificant when compared to radiation pressure from the Sun and the dynamic pressure of the solar wind. The thermosphere in this range has large gradients of pressure, temperature, and composition, and varies greatly due to space weather.

Even so and getting to why Dark Energy exists. A flat Universe, combined with the measured mass density of the Universe and the accelerating expansion of the Universe, indicates that space has non-zero vacuum energy, which is called "Dark Energy".

Unlike matter and dark matter, dark energy seems not to be concentrated in galaxies: although dark energy may account for a majority of the mass energy in the Universe, dark energy's influence is 5 orders of magnitude smaller than the influence of gravity from matter and dark matter within the Milky Way.

As noted before, most scientists think that dark matter is composed of **non-baryonic matter**. The lead candidate is weakly interacting with massive particles. These have ten to a hundred times the mass of a proton, but their weak interactions with "normal" matter make them difficult to detect.

It turns out that 68% **of the universe is dark energy**. Dark matter makes up about 27%. The rest - everything on Earth, everything ever observed with all instruments, all normal matter - adds up to less than 5% of the universe. Some proposals allow for dark energy's density to be changing over time.   If dark energy gets more powerful over time, as some of these observations have suggested, it could tear the universe apart.

And, if all dark matter disappeared, **stars on the edge of galaxies would begin to drift out of the galaxies over time**. Once the gravitational effect of dark matter had fully disappeared (it takes time because gravitons move at the speed of light), stars at the edge would start leaving their host galaxies.

Q: Well, more on that, please. Couldn't God be in dark matter, and exercise his wishes from there? For that matter why is dark matter important and thought to exist?

A: Understanding dark matter is important **to understand the size, shape, and future of the universe**..... Understanding dark matter will also aid in definitively explaining the formation and evolution of galaxies and clusters, but it is a matter of chemistry and reactivity yet to be fully understood.

It does not interact with "baryonic matter" which is matter composed of protons and neutrons that is ordinary matter, as distinct from exotic forms and it is completely invisible to light and other forms of electromagnetic radiation, making dark matter impossible to detect with current instruments. But scientists are confident it exists because of the gravitational effects it has on galaxies and galaxy clusters.

Again, Dark matter makes up a major percentage of all 'stuff' in the universe and is believed to hold the key to interstellar travel, scientists say. Harnessing the weird material will be able to power spaceships at speeds close to the speed of light, according to a new study at the University of Groningen in Holland.

We do know that we exist in that vast chemical-physical realm.

Within it are immense spaces containing particles of matter different than the protons, electrons, etc. that exist in our present understanding of the makeup of matter. Those spaces and their chemistry, nonetheless, are physical/chemical and though the forces so developed have the potential to significantly alter the realm of galaxies.

They are clearly as history reveals not, however, in the business of affecting the empathetic life drive of individual homo sapiens and to any appreciable extent operating to provide providential security of life for homo sapiens.

R: Ok, seeing how massive and reactive all that up there is and recognizing its cataclysmic potential will the universe last forever?

A: The known laws of physics suggest that **by about 10^{100}** (the No. 1 followed by 100 zeros) years from now, star birth will cease, galaxies will go dark, and even black holes will evaporate through a process known as Hawking radiation, leaving little more than simple subatomic particles and energy.

In short, the control we have and can change what happens to each of us, rest solely on each of us. That is, if we exist given the potential of the cosmos to destroy us.

Q: Oh yes, So, so much to know Old Man.! I must run, but can we follow up on this tomorrow.

A: Well, sorry it gets into such detail, but do not want to accidentally misinform you. Yes, see you tomorrow.

Q&A Day 5

Still Looking and Wishing

Back from the divorce lawyer, Someone is sitting at the bench pounding on the seat from time to time and just as the Old Man arrived, he was saying a silent prayer. "Get me out of this." Pretty clear to that senior citizen his friend was troubled. So, he asked. "You know, if this is all too much for you now, we can get back to it later. At that Someone says, no please it helps … putting my mind if you will "In a higher place."

Q: So, God is not in dark space or is not dark energy, right.

A: It looks like that up there as you call it, is everywhere and missioned from starter chemicals to make galaxies and planets and the like. The force is violent way beyond description. But from deep within its chemistry there is reactive force-it does create everything.

R: OK, still can the cosmologist and astrophysicist consider if God exists? That is how in an unlimited cosmos do they explain or accept God?

A: Oh, I see, I think, what you want. I will give you some viewpoints on that. Obviously, the first question is who created the Cosmos, and its Universe (s)?

 Well, many religious persons, including some scientists, hold that **God** created the universe and the various processes driving physical and biological evolution and that these processes then resulted in the creation of galaxies, our solar system, and life on Earth.

Here is an opinion that I will read from a collection via Monica Grady from The Open University, 1st March 2021 *(Monica Grady is a professor of planetary and space science at The Open University)*

If there is a God, would the laws of physics bind them?

I still believed in God (I am now an atheist) when I heard the following question at a seminar, first posed by Einstein, and was stunned by its elegance and depth: "If there is a God who created the entire universe and ALL its laws of physics, does God follow God's own laws? Or can God supersede his own laws, such as traveling faster than the speed of light and thus being able to be in two different places at the same time?"

Could the answer help us prove whether God exists or is this where scientific empiricism and religious faith intersect, with NO true answer? (This is a comment by David Frost, 67, Los Angeles.)

I was in lockdown when I received this question and was instantly intrigued. It is no wonder about the timing-tragic events, such as pandemics, often cause us to question the existence of God: if there is a merciful God, why is a catastrophe like this happening? The idea that God might be "bound" by the laws of physics–which also govern chemistry and biology and thus the limits of medical science – was an interesting one to explore.

If God could not break the laws of physics, she arguably wouldn't be as powerful as you'd expect a supreme being to be. But if she could, why haven't we seen any evidence of the laws of physics ever being broken in the Universe?

To tackle the question, let us break it down a bit. First, can God travel faster than light? Let us just take the question at face value. Light travels at an approximate speed of 3 x 10 to the power of 5 kilometers every second, or 186,000 miles per second (299,500km/s). We learn at school that nothing can travel faster than the speed of light-not even the USS Enterprise in Star Trek when its "Di lithium" crystals are set to max.

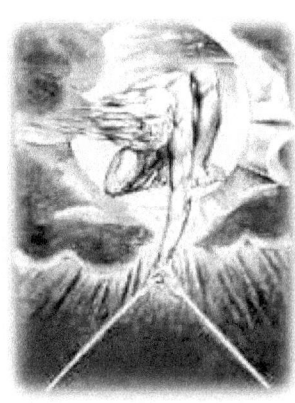

But is it true? A few years ago, a group of physicists posited that particles called tachyons traveled above light speed. Fortunately, their existence as real particles are deemed highly unlikely. If they did exist, they would have an imaginary mass and the fabric of space and time would become distorted leading to violations of causality (and a headache for God).

It seems, so far, that no object has been observed that can travel faster than the speed of light. This in itself does not say anything at all about God. It merely reinforces the knowledge that light travels very fast indeed.

If God exists, one question would be whether that spirit would be bound to the laws of sciences such as physics (Credit: Alamy)

Things get a bit more interesting when you consider how far light has traveled since the beginning. Assuming a traditional big bang cosmology and a light speed of 300,000km/s, then we can calculate that light has traveled 1.3 x 10 x 23 (1.3 times 10 to the power 23) km in the 13.8 billion years of the Universe's existence. Or rather, the observable Universe's existence.

The Universe is expanding at a rate of approximately 70km/s per Mpc (1 Mpc = 1 Megaparsec or 30 billion kilometers), so current estimates suggest the distance to the edge of the universe (if it is such) is 46 billion light-years. As time goes on, the volume of space increases and light must travel for longer to reach us.

In short, there is a lot more universe out there than we can view, but the most distant object that we have seen is a galaxy, GN-z11, that was observed ty the Hubble Space Telescope. This is approximately 1.2 x 10 x 23 km or 13.4 billion light-years away, meaning that it has taken 13.4 billion years for light from the galaxy to reach us. But when the light "set off", the galaxy was only about three billion light-years away from our galaxy, the Milky Way.

As a point to this, many cosmologists believe that the Universe may be part of a more extended cosmos, a multiverse, which the subject is brought in following.

We cannot observe or see across the entirety of the Universe that has grown since the Big Bang because insufficient time has passed for light from the first fractions of a second to reach us. Some argue that we therefore cannot be sure whether the laws of physics could be broken in other cosmic regions–they are just local, accidental laws. And that leads us on to something even bigger than the Universe. "The Multiverse."

The proposition is that the Universe may be part of a more extended cosmos, where many different universes co-exist but do not interact. The idea of the multiverse is backed by the theory of inflation- the idea that the universe expanded hugely before it was 10^{-32} seconds old. Inflation is an important theory because it can explain why the Universe has the shape and structure that we see around us.

But if inflation could happen once, why not many times? We know from experiments that quantum fluctuations can give rise to pairs of particles suddenly coming into existence, only to disappear moments later. And if such fluctuations can produce particles, why not entire atoms, or universes? It has been suggested during the period of chaotic inflation, not everything was happening at the same rate–quantum fluctuations in the expansion could have produced bubbles that blew up to become universes in their own right.

But how does God fit into the multiverse? One headache for cosmologists has been the fact that our Universe seems fine-tuned for life to exist. The fundamental particles created in the Big Bang had the correct properties to enable the formation of hydrogen and deuterium i.e., substances that produced the first stars.

Then, the question arises could quantum physics help explain a God that could be in two places at once? (Credit: Nasa)

The physical laws governing nuclear reactions in these stars then produced the stuff that lives made of carbon, nitrogen, and oxygen. How come all the physical laws and parameters in the universe happen to have the values that allowed stars, planets, and life to develop?

Some argue it is just a lucky coincidence. Others say we should not be surprised to see biofriendly physical laws-they produced us, so what else would we see? Some theists, however, argue it points to the existence of a God creating favorable conditions.

But God is not a valid scientific explanation. The theory of the multiverse, instead, solves the mystery because it allows different universes to have different physical laws. So, it is not surprising that we should happen to see ourselves in one of the few universes that could support life. Of course, you cannot disprove the idea that a God may have created the multiverse.

If two particles are entangled, you automatically manipulate its partner when you manipulate it

This is all very hypothetical, and one of the biggest criticisms of theories of the multiverse is that because there seem to have been no interactions between our Universe and other universes, then the notion of the multiverse cannot be directly evaluated.

Quantum weirdness

Now let us consider whether God can be in more than one place at the same time. Much of the science and technology we use in space science is based on the counter-intuitive theory of the tiny world of atoms and particles known as quantum mechanics (popularly "Quantum Weirdness").

The theory enables something called quantum entanglement: spookily connected particles. If two particles are entangled, you automatically manipulate their partner when you manipulate it, even if they are very far apart and without the two interacting. There are better descriptions of entanglement than the one I give here–but this is simple enough that I can follow it.

Imagine a particle that decays into two sub-particles, A and B. The properties of the sub-particles must add up to the properties of the original particle-this is the principle of conservation. For example, all particles have a quantum property called "spin"-roughly, they move as if they were tiny compass needles. If the original particle has a "spin" of zero, one of the two sub-particles must have a positive spin and the other a negative spin, which means that each of A and B has a 50% chance of having a positive or a negative spin. (According to quantum mechanics, particles are in a mix of different states until you measure them.)

Albert Einstein described quantum entanglement as "spooky action at a distance"

The properties of A and B are not independent of each other – they are entangled–even if located in separate laboratories on separate planets. If you measure the spin of A and you find it to be positive, then imagine a friend measured the spin of B while you measured A. For the principle of conservation to work, she must find the spin of B to be negative.

But – and this is where things become murky–like sub-particle A, B had a 50:50 chance of being positive, so its spin state "became" negative at the time that the spin state of A was measured as positive. In other words, information about the spin state was transferred between the two sub-particles instantly. Such transfer of quantum information happens faster than the speed of light. Given that Einstein himself described quantum entanglement as "spooky action at a distance", I think all of us can be forgiven for finding this a bizarre effect.

We now know there is something faster than the speed of light. This is-quantum information. Atomic Particles have "spin states" information about the spin state must be transferred between the two sub-particles instantly This does not prove or disprove God, but it can help us think of God in physical terms-maybe as a shower of entangled particles, transferring quantum information back and forth, and so occupying many places at the same time? Even many universes at the same time?

Science requires proof, religious belief requires faith.

So, from this one can have an image of God keeping galaxy-sized plates spinning while juggling planet-sized balls-tossing bits of information from one teetering universe to another, to keep everything in motion. Fortunately, God can multitask- keeping the fabric of space and time in operation. All that is required is a little faith!

Has this essay come close to answering the questions posed? I suspect not: if you believe in God, then the idea of God is bound by the laws of physics is nonsense, because God can do everything, even travel faster than light. If you do not believe in God, then the question is equally nonsensical, because there is not a God, and nothing can travel faster than light.

This is indeed where science and religion differ. Science requires proof, religious belief requires faith. Scientists do not try to prove or disprove God's existence because they know there is not an experiment that can ever detect God. And if you believe in God, it does not matter what scientists discover about the Universe-any cosmos can be thought of as being consistent with God.

Our views of God, physics, or anything else depends on perspective. But let us end with a quotation from a truly authoritative source. No, it is not the Bible. Nor is it a cosmology textbook. It is from a "Good Reads (Reaper Man) book show and by Terry Pratchett:

"Light thinks it travels faster than anything, but it is wrong. No matter how fast light travels, it finds the darkness has always got there first and is waiting for it." (actually, if one thinks this through one realized that the darkness was already positioned there).

R: Thanks much for taking me through that, but no matter. But it is very clear, with all that to run, all that existing, nothing in that tells me that the God I need is at all concerned about me or you or anyone else.

Q: So, let us get back down to me (or you or anyone else on this planet, for Pete's Sake!). Was I, you, or anyone in the past created by a spiritual force? You know who I am talking about that is the God who will rescue me and take me away to a safe place.

A: Ok we will share information on that next time. Do realize that is a very difficult question. It has to do with what you are, how you came about, and what is within.

See you here in the a.m.

Q&A Day 6

The Genesis of Life

Morning brought the old man to the bench before Someone arrived. He had two cups of coffee, but they were barely warm when Someone showed up. "Sorry, got in a tangle with my son. He called me a poop-head-deserter, because of the divorce. Had to calm him down before taking him to school so we were late. Honestly, I do not believe I can make it out of this mess. Need advice, support higher than the #$@% Lawyer.

Q: Sorry, let us back up! Even so, I do want to follow up on how I was created (and of course, I do not mean via sex). I mean that cosmos bit is so full of violence it cannot explain me and you and all the others, being born from it, can it?

A: Ok, if you want to get "down to earth" we can go there, but it is not just a simple matter of opening the bible or the Quran or other holy books. It does have to do with vast times and special chemical creations. There are miracles and we can open to them after a bit of exploration.

The story of our earth creation, more to the point- we as created on earth centers on the formation and existence of "Nucleic Acids, DNA (Deoxyribose Nucleic Acid) and RNA (a ribose Nucleic Acid).

Michael Marshalls, "Earth." Reminds us that DNA is the foundation for an answer to your question. It has been shown it has existed long before life itself. (Article, 22 August 2012)

There has been some argument about its genesis. Even though DNA is the essential molecule to all life on Earth, some biologists think that life began with RNA. Just like DNA, it stores genetic information. RNA can fold into complex shapes that can clamp onto other molecules and speed up chemical reactions, just like a protein, and it is structurally simpler than DNA, so that might be easier to make at first.

However, Scientists are close to demonstrating that the building blocks of DNA can form spontaneously from chemicals thought to be present on the primordial Earth. Obviously then whatever the conversion pathway to DNA its existence as a molecule could have predated the birth of life.

And starting with a mix of chemicals present on the early Earth, scientists indeed, have created a sugar-like that in DNA, (*Journal of the American Chemical Society*, doi.org/h6q).

So, it is apparent that precursor DNA nucleotides were naturally present in the environment. Primitive chemical associations "organisms" would take them up and use them in their reactions, later developing the tools to make their own DNA once it became clear how advantageous the molecule was.

Early organisms must have scavenged for materials in this way, says Mathew Levy of the Albert Einstein College of Medicine in New York City. "The early Earth was probably a bloody mess," he says, with all manner of rich pickings on offer. There is nothing to tell us exactly how and when life first used DNA. However, "It almost becomes a choose-your-own-adventure game," says Levy. That is, it certainly occurred early in Earth History and began among the billions of reactions occurring as the planet struggled to become "Earth."

Nevertheless, all living things have DNA within their cells. In fact, every cell in a multicellular organism possesses the full set of DNA required for that organism. In other words, whenever organisms reproduce, a portion of their DNA is passed along to their offspring.

Q: OK, I am getting the idea, I think. Living creatures require "DNA" to exist and it can be created through chemical reactions from chemicals that were created or available here on earth in its early formation. Is that the case?

A: Yes, that is the central point. So that leads to the "Launch"! Here is more from a recent description summarized many times in 2020 reports.

There was a 'Land Start." Some of the key evidence in favor of this idea emerged in 2009 when scientist Sutherland announced that he and his team had successfully made two of the four nucleotides that comprise RNA. They started with phosphate and four simple carbon-based chemicals, including a cyanide salt called cyanamide. The chemicals were dissolved in water throughout, but they were highly concentrated, and crucial steps required UV radiation. Such reactions could not take place deep in an ocean-only in a small pool or stream exposed to sunlight, where chemicals could be concentrated, he says.

Sutherland's team has since shown that the same starter chemicals if they are treated subtly differently, can also produce precursors to proteins and lipids. The researchers suggest that these reactions might have taken place if water containing cyanide salts was dried out by the Sun, leaving a layer of dry, cyanide-related chemicals that was then heated by, say, geothermal activity. His team has produced the building blocks of DNA-something previously thought implausible-using energy from sunlight and some of the same chemicals at high concentrations.

This approach has been extended by biochemist Moran Frenkel-Pinter at the NSF–NASA Center for Chemical Evolution in Atlanta, Georgia, and her colleagues. They showed that amino acids spontaneously linked up to form protein-like chains if they were dried out._And those kinds of reactions were more likely to occur with the 20 amino acids found in proteins today, compared with other amino acids. That means intermittent drying could help to explain why life uses only those amino acids, out of hundreds of possibilities. "We saw selection for today's amino acids," says Frenkel-Pinter.

Wet and dry. Intermittent drying out can also help to drive these molecular building blocks to assemble into more-complex, life-like structures.

A classic experiment along these lines was published in 1982 by researchers David Deamer and Gail Barchfeld, then at the University of California, Davis. Their aim was to study how lipids, another class of long-chain molecules, self-organize to form the membranes that surround cells. They first made vesicles: spherical blobs with a watery core surrounded by two lipid layers. Then the researchers dried the vesicles, and the lipids reorganized into a multi-layered structure like a stack of pancakes. Strands of DNA, previously floating in the water, became trapped between the layers. When the researchers added water again, the vesicles reformed with DNA inside them. This was a step towards a simple cell!

One very likely scenario about the origin of life suggests it started around vents on the seafloor that spew hot alkaline waters. "These wet-dry cycles are everywhere," says Deamer (University of California, Santa Cruz). "It's as simple as rainwater evaporating on wet rocks." But when they are applied to biological chemicals such as lipids, he says, remarkable things happen.

In a 2008 study, Deamer and his team mixed nucleotides and lipids with water, then put them through wet-dry cycles. When the lipids formed layers, the nucleotides linked up into RNA-like chains — a reaction that would not happen in water unaided.

Other studies point also to another factor that is a key part of life's origins: light.

That is one of the conclusions coming from the team of synthetic biologist Jack Szostak at Massachusetts General Hospital in Boston, which works with 'protocells'-simple versions of cells that contain a handful of chemicals, but can grow, compete, and replicate themselves. The protocells display more-lifelike behaviors if they are exposed to conditions like those on land. One study, on which Adamala was a co- author, found that the protocells could use energy from light to divide, in a simple form of reproduction. Similarly, Claudia Bonfio, now also at the MRC Laboratory of Molecular Biology, and her colleagues showed in 2017 that UV radiation drives the synthesis of iron-sulfur clusters, which are crucial to many proteins. These include those in the electron transport chain, which helps to power all living cells by driving the synthesis of the energy-storage molecule ATP. The iron-sulfur clusters would break apart if they were exposed to water, but Bonfio's team found they were more stable if the clusters were surrounded by simple peptides 3–12 amino acids long.

Water, but not too much

Such studies have given momentum to the idea that life began on a well-lit surface with a limited amount of water. Like Deamer, Frenkel-Pinter argues that wet-dry cycles were crucial. Dry conditions, she says, provided an opportunity for chain molecules such as proteins and Nucleic Acids to form.

But simply making RNA and other molecules is not life. A self-sustaining, dynamic system must form. Frenkel-Pinter suggests that water's destructiveness could have helped to drive that. Just as prey animals evolved to run faster or secrete toxins to survive predators, the first biological molecules might have evolved to cope with water's chemical attacks — and even to harness its reactivity for good.

In a study at Hell's Gate hot springs near Rotorua, New Zealand, samples from hydrothermal pools went through cycles of drying and rewetting, which promoted chemical reactions that produced RNA-like molecules. (Credit: Westend61/Getty)

Frenkel-Pinter's team followed up on its previous study_showing that drying caused amino acids to link up spontaneously. The team found that their proto proteins could interact with RNA and that both became more stable in water as a result. In effect, the water acted as a selection pressure:

only those combinations of molecules that could survive in water would continue because the others would be destroyed.

The idea is that, with each cycle of wetting, the weaker molecules, or those that could not protect themselves by binding to others, were destroyed. Bonfio and her team demonstrated this in a study in which they attempted to convert simple fatty acids into more-complex lipids resembling those found in modern cell membranes. The researchers created mixtures of lipids and found that the simple ones were destroyed by water, while the larger, more complex ones accumulated. "At some point, you would have enough of these lipids for them to form membranes," she says. In other words, there might be a Goldilocks amount of water: not so much that biological molecules are destroyed too quickly, but not so little that nothing changes.

So, net-net there have been many studies that the molecules needed for our life and other living creatures here on earth were generated early in earth history right here on earth!

Q: Hey. that is a lot of research. Thanks for showing me the path. To put it straight forward, once the earth formed the ingredients necessary to create molecules for life were available and conditions on this planet could cook them into our living creations. Right?

A: Yes, that was one very likely path and even though the chemistry may differ from one scientific study to another the outcome has been us and virtually all life on earth.

R: Ok, so I see why I am here on earth. From hard cold space, we are hereby natural chemical-physical genesis.

Q: But I am still worried and need answers. I want to live on and have that spirit (God) take care of me Now! I mean cannot I at least be regenerated, or even reincarnated somewhere else.

Hmmm. we will talk about that - wading into it tomorrow if that is OK.

Yes, I will be there if my ex-wife and son do not shoot me first!

Q&A Day 7

Other Places for Life (Multiverse)?

The next day arrives threatening to rain again after a bit of sprinkling. Someone is sitting on the bench, cussing, as usual, a wet newspaper in hand it is just being used as an emergency headcover. The Old man arrives in a raincoat and with his briefcase closed having put the needed pictures and articles safely inside. He offers a coffee and a pleasant "Good Morning." Someone takes the coffee sits it beside on the bench and then in a surprisingly loud voice, starts off the day.

Q: Ok, OK! So, in net, there is this vast cosmos, that it seems is in a design that may not specifically "house" the God I believe in. But in all of that is there only one universe, one place where I could be risen or re-risen to live on while I get the blazes out of this mess. You have said something the other day about a Multiverse, but to get to your question, really are we searching for an "Earth-Like" planet. We have life, but are we the only planet with such ability? What makes Earth unique from the other planets? Can we go elsewhere?

A: There is that possibility, that is, it can be conceived of, but there are several questions behind this. I will try to give you some insight.

To begin Earth is **special because it is an ocean planet**. Water covers 70% of the Earth's surface. Earth's atmosphere is made mostly of nitrogen and has plenty of oxygen for us to breathe. And our atmosphere protects us from incoming meteoroids, most of which break up before they can hit the surface. (Article, Jul 19, 2021)

So, with some security and some provisions what conditions made life possible on Earth and no other planets? Well, it is **the right distance from the Sun, it is protected from harmful solar radiation by its magnetic field**, it is kept warm by an insulating atmosphere, and it has the right chemical ingredients for life, including water and carbon.

R: I did not really get that. What is the main way Earth is potentially different from other planets?

It could be different from the other planets **because it has liquid water on its surface, maintains life, and has active plate movement**. It rotates on its axis every 24 hours (a day) and revolves around the Sun every 365 days (a year). The Earth has one moon.

Q: Ok, but all of us know from the news that there are other planets, Right? How do we know there is not one that has those properties?

A: Ok, here is information from Computer Systems Senior Engineer, Valdis Kletnieks. (1989-present)

We have found over 3,000 exoplanets now, and a *lot* of them are in their respective star's "Goldilocks Zone" something like 20%. This is the zone that is considered not too hot and not too cold and just the right size for life as we know it to evolve

Now, whether these planets have enough mass to hold a suitable atmosphere and a magnetic field strong enough, and enough water, etc. etc. etc., is still an open question.

And, other Scientists Estimate 20 Billion Earth-Like Planets in Our Galaxy

The following is via Scott Neuman. A new study suggests there could be far more Earth-like planets orbiting distant stars than once thought, some of which might even harbor life.

A team of astronomers from the University of California, Berkeley, and the University of Hawaii at Manoa, Honolulu, used the Kepler space telescope to survey 42,000 Sun-like stars looking for a telltale dimming caused by an orbiting planet as it crosses between us and the parent star.

While the method is not new, in the past it has tended to favor finding larger planets orbiting close in lots of so-called "Hot Jupiter's" that are too big and/or way too close to their stars to be candidates for life. Kepler's main mission has been to find planets in the Goldilocks Zone-right for life to evolve.

The team publishing in an issue of PNAS (www.pnas.org)_ looked at how frequently the dimming took place to determine the orbital period-and, therefore, the distance from the star -as well as how much light was blocked, which gives an indication of the size of the planet: "We found 603 planets, 10 of which are Earth-size and orbit in the habitable zone, where conditions permit surface liquid water," the team writes. "We find that 22 percent of Sun-like stars harbor Earth-size planets orbiting in their habitable zones. The nearest such planet may be within 12 light-years."

In the "Smithsonian" there is information that "over the past 18 years, astronomers have discovered 1038 planets orbiting distant stars.

Disappointingly, though, the vast majority don't seem like candidates to support life as we know it—they're either so close to their home star that all water would likely evaporate, or so far away that all of it would freeze, or they're made up of gas instead of rock and more closely resemble our solar system's gas giants than Earth."

Andrew Howard, one of the study's co-authors, enthused at a recent news conference that their 22 percent figure means that "with about 100 billion stars in our Milky Way galaxy, that's about 20 billion such planets. That is a few Earth-sized planets for every human being on the planet Earth."

And that is just in a single galaxy. If the figure for potentially habitable planets derived by the team of scientists is correct, we could take a minor flight of fancy and multiply the 20 billion planets by about 500 billion galaxies in the observable universe for a truly astronomical number – possibly 1,000 trillion Earth-like planets.

Q: Well, all that is pretty darn impressive, Old Man. Maybe offers some choices?

A: Yes, that addresses potential and some limitations, but there is more to describe.

Ethan Siegel points out why some believe that the multiverse must exist.

The multiverse idea states that there are an arbitrarily large number of Universes like our own out there, ... Look out toward the sky at the Universe all you want, with arbitrarily powerful technology, and you'll never find an edge!

Space goes on as far as we can see, and everywhere we look we see the

same things: matter and radiation. In all directions, we find the same telltale signs of an expanding Universe: the leftover radiation from a hot, dense state; galaxies that evolve in size, mass, and number; elements that change abundances as stars live and die.

But what lies beyond our observable Universe? Is there an abyss of nothingness beyond the light signals that could reach us since the Big Bang? Is there just more Universe like our own, out there past our observational limits? Or is there a Multiverse, mysterious in nature and forever unable to be seen?

Unless there is something seriously wrong with our understanding of the Universe, the Multiverse must be the answer. Here is why.

Yes, The Multiverse is an extremely controversial idea, but at its core, it is a very simple concept. Just as the Earth does not occupy a special position in the Universe, nor does the Sun, the Milky Way, or any other location, the Multiverse goes a step farther and claims that there is nothing special about the entire visible Universe.

The Multiverse is the idea that our Universe, and all that is contained within it, is just one small part of a larger structure. This larger entity encapsulates our observable Universe as a small part of a larger Universe that extends beyond the limits of our observations. That entire structure — the unobservable Universe — may itself be part of a larger spacetime that includes many other, disconnected Universes, which may or may not be like the Universe we inhabit.

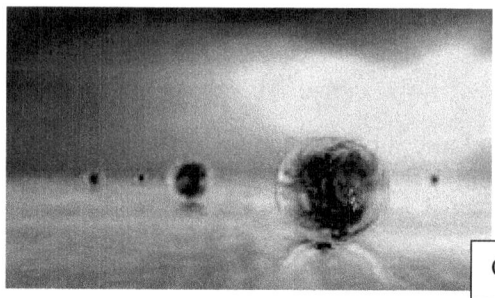

This is an illustration of multiple, independent Universes, causally disconnected from one another in an ever-forever cosmos.

Ozytive / Public Domain

If this is the idea of the Multiverse, I can understand your skepticism at the notion that we could somehow know whether it does or does not exist. Physics and astronomy are sciences that rely on measurable, experimental, or otherwise observational confirmation. If we are looking for evidence of something that exists outside of our visible Universe and leaves no trace within it, the idea of a Multiverse is fundamentally untestable.

But there are all sorts of things that we cannot observe that we know must be true. Decades before we directly detected gravitational waves, we knew that they must exist, because we observed their effects. Binary pulsars — spinning neutron stars orbiting around one another — were observed to have their revolutionary periods shortened. Something must be carrying energy away, and that

While we certainly welcomed the confirmation that tools such as Virgo provided for gravitational waves via direct detection, we already knew that they needed to exist because of this indirect evidence. Those who would argue that indirect evidence is no indicator of gravitational waves might still be unconvinced that binary pulsars emit them; LIGO and Virgo did not see the gravitational waves they came from

So, if we cannot observe the Multiverse directly, what indirect evidence do we have for its existence? How do we know that there is a more unobservable Universe beyond the part we can observe, and how do we know that what we call our Universe is likely just one of many embedded in the Multiverse?

We look to the Universe itself and draw conclusions about its nature based on what observations about it reveal.

When we look out to the edge of the observable Universe, we find that the light rays emitted from the earliest times from the Cosmic-Microwave Background make patterns on the sky. These patterns not only reveal the density and temperature fluctuations that the Universe was born with, as

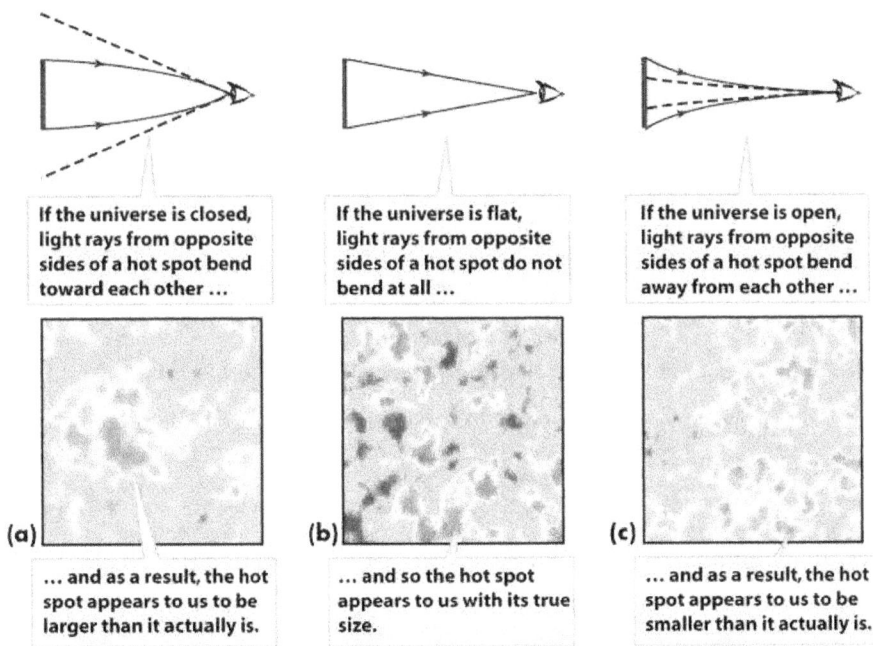

If the universe is closed, light rays from opposite sides of a hot spot bend toward each other ...

If the universe is flat, light rays from opposite sides of a hot spot do not bend at all ...

If the universe is open, light rays from opposite sides of a hot spot bend away from each other ...

(a)

(b)

(c)

... and as a result, the hot spot appears to us to be larger than it actually is.

... and so the hot spot appears to us with its true size.

... and as a result, the hot spot appears to us to be smaller than it actually is.

well as the matter and energy composition of the Universe, but also the geometry of space itself.

We can conclude from this that space is not positively curved (like a sphere) or negatively curved (like a saddle), but rather spatially flat, indicating that the unobservable Universe likely extends far beyond the part we can access. It never curves back on itself, it never repeats, and it has no empty gaps in it. If it is curved, it has a diameter that's hundreds of times greater than the part we can see.

That might indicate that there is a more unobservable Universe beyond the part of our Universe we can access, but it does not prove it, and it does not provide evidence for a Multiverse. There are, however, two concepts in physics that have been established far beyond a reasonable doubt: cosmic inflation and quantum physics.

Cosmic inflation is the theory that gave rise to the hot Big Bang. Rather than beginning with a singularity, there is a physical limit to how hot and how dense the initial, early stages of our expanding Universe could have reached. If we had achieved arbitrarily high temperatures in the past, there would be clear signatures that aren't there:

- large-amplitude temperature fluctuations early on,

- seed density fluctuations limited by the scale of the cosmic horizon,

- and leftover, high-energy relics from early times, like magnetic monopoles.

These signatures are all missing!

The temperature fluctuations are at the 0.003% level; the density fluctuations exceed the scale of the cosmic horizon; the limits on monopoles and other relics are incredibly stringent. The fact that these signatures are not there has an enormous implication to them: the Universe never reached those arbitrarily high temperatures. Something else came before the hot Big Bang to set it up.

That is where cosmic inflation comes in. Theorized in the early 1980s, it was designed to solve many puzzles with the Big Bang, but did what you'd hope for any new physical theory: it made measurable, testable predictions for observable signatures that would appear within our Universe.

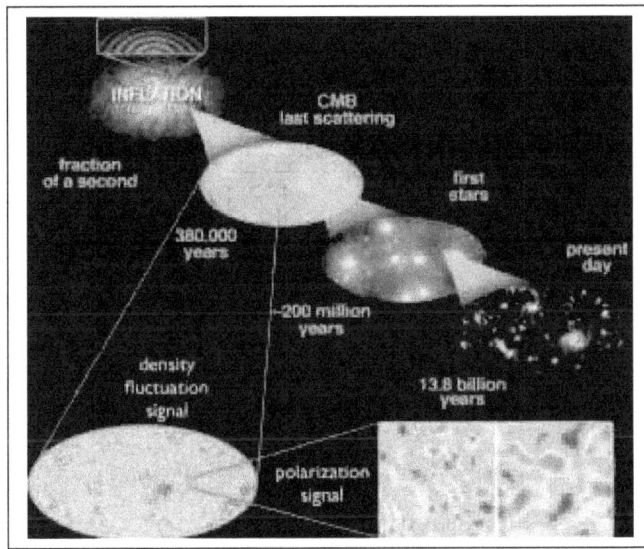

We see the predicted lack of the spatial curvature; we see an adiabatic nature to the fluctuations the Universe was born with; and we have detected a spectrum and magnitude of initial fluctuations that jibe with inflation's predictions; we have seen the super-horizon fluctuations that inflation predicts must arise.

We may not know everything about inflation, but we do have a very strong suite of evidence that supports a period in the early Universe where it occurred. It set up and gave rise to the Big Bang and predicts a set and spectrum of fluctuations that gave rise to the seeds of structure that grew into the cosmic web we observe today. Only inflation gives us predictions for our Universe that match what we observe.

"So, big deal," you might say. "You took a small region of space, you allowed inflation to expand it to some very large volume, and our observable, visible Universe is contained within that volume. Even if this is all right, this only tells us that our unobservable Universe extends far beyond the visible part. You haven't established the Multiverse at all."

And all of that would be correct. But remember, there is one more ingredient we need to add in: quantum physics.

This is the key point that tells us why a Multiverse is inevitable! Where inflation ends right away, we get a hot Big Bang and a large Universe, where a small part of it might be like our own observable Universe. But there are other regions, outside of the region where it ends, where inflation continues for longer.

Where the quantum spreading occurs in just the right fashion, inflation might end there, too, giving rise to a hot Big Bang and an even larger Universe, where a small portion might be like our observable Universe.

But the other regions are not still just inflating, they are also growing. You can calculate the rate at which the inflating regions grow and compare them to the rate at which new Universes form and hot Big Bangs occur. In all cases where inflation gives you predictions that match the observed Universe, we grow new Universes and newly inflating regions faster than inflation can come to an end. This picture, of huge Universes, far bigger than the meager part that's observable to us, constantly being created across this exponentially inflating space, is what the Multiverse is all about.

It is not a new, testable scientific prediction, but rather a theoretical consequence that's unavoidable, based on the laws of physics as they're understood today. Whether the laws of physics are identical to our own in those other Universes is unknown.

If you have an inflationary Universe that is governed by quantum physics, a Multiverse is unavoidable.

 As always, we are collecting as much new, compelling evidence as we can continue to better understand the entire cosmos. It may turn out that inflation is wrong, that quantum physics is wrong, or that applying these rules the way we do has some fundamental flaw.

But so far, everything adds up. Unless we have gotten something wrong, the Multiverse is inevitable, and the Universe we inhabit is just a minuscule part of it.

Q: Old man that all is just so much proposing back and forth. But to put it in a few words… there is the possibility of other places where life and even ours might inhabit. Yes?

Seems the bottom line here is where my soul can become so it can be launched to heaven. Yes?

A: Well, OK. However, it is important to note that your last concern raises more questions, and the information could be challenging. Let us get into that next time though. OK. What say next Monday.

Q&A Day 8

The Soul and Regeneration of Me

PQ: there was surely a spirit that made us. And I have a soul too?

After the weekend, our two, new acquaintances, but now trusting friends, meet once again on that bench. Someone looked more disheveled and worried than before, clearly, he had another crazy time with his ex and his son. The Old man handed the coffee, and as he sat down, patted Someone tactfully on the shoulder, commenting "It is OK if we just sit. I am here to listen if you want to share.

R: Thanks friend but there is no sense in taking anyone else into my mess. The main t. g here is my concern about myself.

Q: Can I get my soul to become somewhere else, You know if I die could I and my soul be regenerated … reincarnated in one of those other places, a different galaxy, and the planet.

A: OK, let us investigate it, but do be aware this may be a most difficult subject.

. Hindu philosophers tell us that the soul of a person who has attained *moksha* (liberation from the cycle of re-birth) unites with God (the Atman).

These philosophies hold that in the meantime, they are reborn on earth, and conditionally even as various earth creatures. Or in other faiths in a haven as angelic spirits.

So is such reincarnation possible from a scientific, rationalist point of view?

Let us begin, for the sake of argument, by saying that when you get right down to it everything, consists of quantum particles. These particles can as well be in one place as another, even at the same time. As Wikipedia informs us: *The Everett many-worlds interpretation, formulated in 1956, holds that all the possibilities described by quantum theory simultaneously occur in a "multiverse" composed of mostly independent parallel universes.*

The crucial word here is "simultaneously." Everything can be thought of as being in no place at any time. That is because places and times are concepts, we bring with us to the quantum level. They do not seem to exist there. Or if they do, they are created only in the act of our applying them, and our measurements have meaning to us but not to them.

What, you may well ask, is a quantum string? Here Wikipedia is a model of clarity: *A string is one of the main objects of study in string theory, a branch of theoretical physics. There are different string theories, many of which are unified by M-theory. A string is an object with a one-dimensional spatial extent, unlike an elementary particle which is zero-dimensional, or point-like.*

And what is one-dimensional, as opposed to zero-dimensional? My layman's rule of thumb is that if something has no dimensions, then it is nothing. Obviously, I am naive. So, let us turn to one-dimensional strings, which now seem as tangible as a cantaloupe compared to zero-dimensional particles. At least there is something there. It is, as you may have guessed, very small. It is no larger than the Planck length. What size is a Planck length? I quote: *Current theory suggests that one Planck length is the smallest distance or size about which anything can be known.*

In other words, if they ever find something smaller than the Planck length, then *that* will be the Planck length. When we laypeople refer to something's "distance or size," we think we are describing two different things, i.e.: *The large dog is ten feet away from me.* No, that would be its distance *and* size. At the quantum level, distance and size might as well be each other. To cut to the chase: **Everything could well be anywhere, and at the same time-by string quantum theory.**

This begins to sound suspiciously like the **Ether**, defined by medieval magicians **as a fifth element flowing through the universe.** We learn from the philosophy of Matthew Rees: *Ether is very versatile and can be transformed into matter, energy, or even essence by spells... a spell does not detect the *presence* of ether, since ether is everywhere; it detects disturbances in the pattern or flow of ether.*

These disturbances sound something like the **gravitational effect by which quantum particles are said to make their presence known.** If the Ether can be transformed into either matter or energy, then magicians were there before Einstein, and E=m2 can be thought of as a spell.

Both quantum particles and the Ether can be considered in general terms to be that which is everywhere and Everything.

Now we get to the point. You may have seen this coming. We, ourselves, consist entirely in and of this material. Our identities, our

names, our personalities, our beliefs, opinions, senses of humor--indeed, what we think of as our minds. We consist of one-dimensional bits of the cosmic total. And we might just as well be *different bits*--elsewhere--because the "self" is an organizing principle which we have imposed upon this chaos. If you were to stand back far away from us, we would appear to be a no-dimensional point, but as you draw closer, we are revealed to be a great deal more than that!

Therefore, our identities were assembled from this quantum material, or Ether, by the organizing principle of our conception of ourselves. We bring ourselves into being. Our consciousness is the gravitation. We came from whirling nothing; we return to whirling nothing. The "dust" as the expression goes, we came from and the "dust" to which we return is not there but thinking makes it so.

These bits might as comfortably be at the other end of the universe as to where they are. Only by the act of regarding them do we hold them together. You assemble your bits, I assemble mine, and when we cease thinking they all fly back into the general pool of Everything, Everywhere.

Thus, you and I temporarily consist of ourselves, and someday might consist of other-selves or other things. We will be back, but a precious lot of good it will do us, because we will not know it. So, yes, reincarnation is possible from a rationalist, scientific point of view.

We have been and will be reincarnated as part of the vast store of everything there is. We will be suns, moon, stars, rain. Look for us in the weather reports.

If I am closing on a vague (challenging-realistic) note, consider my difficulties in determining where to stand and what to regard. I am inside my mind--trapped here, for as long as I can remember. The fact that you exist is only (in the vast ether) hearsay evidence. It makes life more interesting for me to think so. I would not want my mind to experience only an infinitely spinning formless void when it is better employed by thinking of the actor Meryl Streep.

OK Old Man I get it in terms of Cosmos Chemicals we are subatomic dust. Once congealed we make ourselves from it.

But that being accomplished in one's minds and daily physical life, what about our (my, dam 'it) soul. That is what I am most concerned about, I want it --Providence helping me now, and in Heaven, wherever that is.

Ok, there are a good many comments, papers, etc. on this. But the one I just gave you and we will read takes the matter back to the brain. It is by Sunil K. Pandya. The title "The Soul and the Structure of the Brain Understanding Brain, Mind and Soul: Contributions from Neurology and Neurosurgery."

It starts with a comment by Otto Rank (2002) who has summed up the situation regards the soul. He felt that belief in the soul grew out of the need to reassure ourselves of immortality, despite our knowledge of the immutable biological fact of death: 'The collision (between our need and the fact of death) created a spark in our individual and social consciousness that through history has become both consolation and inspiration: the immortal soul... The immortal soul, whether fact or fiction, gives comfort.'

V. S. Ramachandran, a brain scientist at the University of California, San Diego, is less tactful. He said in an interview that there might be a soul in the sense of 'the universal spirit of the cosmos,' but the soul as it is usually spoken of, 'an immaterial spirit that occupies individual brains and that only evolved in humans—all that is complete nonsense.' Belief in that kind of soul 'is basically superstition/"

For scientists who are people of faith, like Kenneth R. Miller, a biologist at Brown University, asking about the science of the soul is pointless, in a way, because it is not a subject science can address. 'It is not physical and investigable in the world of science,' he said. Dr. Miller said he spoke often at college campuses and elsewhere and was regularly asked, 'What do you say as a scientist about the soul?' His answer, he said, is always the same: 'As a scientist, I have nothing to say about the soul. It is not a scientific idea' (Dean, 2007).

If there be a soul, where is it located? The views of neuroscientists are as follows.

If we accept the existence of the soul and its localization in the brain, we must focus on the brainstem. Christopher Pallis (1983), discussing the definition of whole-brain death, provided a modern concept of the soul. 'The loss of the capacity for consciousness and of the capacity to breathe (after brain death) relate to functional disturbances at the opposite ends of the brain stem while the former is also a meaningful alternative to "the departure of the soul".'

Greenfield's (1997) description is relevant. The soul, like the seat of consciousness (in its neurological sense) lies in 'the cocktail of brain soup and spark' within the deep cerebrum and brainstem, whence dopamine, noradrenaline, acetylcholine is released 'in a fountain-like arrangement onto the more sophisticated regions of the (cerebral) cortex and immediate subcortical structures' to produce a series of electrical and chemical events.

We must confess that the existence of the soul remains unproven by tests 'in the acid baths of experiment and logic.' Nor has it 'enjoyed repeated vindication' (Wilson, 1998). Despite all that has been written on the soul, it is difficult to fault Musil's observation published in 1990: '(There is) an abiding miscommunication between the intellect and the soul. We do not have too much intellect and too little soul, but too little intellect in matters of the soul.'

We shall eventually come to conclusions like those reached by Sir Thomas Browne (19 October 1605–19 October 1682) in his most famous work, the *Religio Medici*:

'Amongst all those rare discoveries and curious pieces, I find in the Fabric of Man, there is no Organ or Instrument for the rational Soul; for in the brain there is not anything of a moment more than I can discover in the cranny of a beast, and this is an argument of the inorganity of the Soul. Thus, we are men, and we know not how; there is something in us that can be without us, and will be after us; though, strangely, it hath no history what it was before us, nor cannot tell how it entered in us' (Browne, 1635/2009).

We remain 'children of Tantalus, frustrated by the failure to grasp that which seems within reach…' (Wilson, 1998).

Of course, if you have a hyperactive funny bone, you could paraphrase Woody Allen, who, as so often, has the ultimate comic word on the subject: 'You cannot prove the non-existence of the soul; you just have to take it on faith.' (http://cavett.blogs.nytimes.com/2007/02/07/ghost-stories/?apage=3)

In short-the soul is DNA-based… creates the brain which creates the soul!

R: Whew Old man, you have really pushed me to the ground. Now I have no hope!

A: Not the case! Can you rest a bit, Go home hug your son and tell your ex. that you all (and I mean you working with them) will work things out?

And I hope you can make it tomorrow, where a different direction is available.

R: Ok, you can bet I will be there!

Q&A Day 9

Choices in Light of the Day

When we look down on the two at the bench, we see Someone looking at the Old Man with an angry face. Ok, I made things a bit better at home, son loved my "soft" approach to his Mom. But now you have pilled upon me information that gives me no hope. I cannot see where heaven is, and I am worried about God not helping me through the mess of my life.

A: OK, I can see your worries, but we are looking at things differently. You are looking for Miracles. Here are the definitions of that.

The Miracle

1. A surprising and welcome event that is not explicable by natural or scientific laws and is therefore considered to be the work of a divine agency. As and "the miracle of rising from the grave".

2. A highly improbable or extraordinary event, development, or accomplishment that brings very welcome consequences." It was a miracle that more people had not been killed or injured"

3. An amazing product or achievement, or an outstanding example of something "a machine which was a miracle of design."

We have discussed in fact covered in detail all three of these. The First would apply to an action by a God or Atman. In no way has this been ignored. What has been said is that it is not testable by rational scientific means. However, except for its influence (1) on us, as individuals may choose, we in effect are made capable to move on because of the cosmic reality, which is observable, scientifically testable, and when carefully considered amounts to miracles of type 2 and 3.

Yes, Miracles! Here you are an absolutely awesome creation, derived after billions of earth formations from the tremendous explosions of cosmic chemicals. *That is reality!*

This reality of the existence of everything, in fact, releases you!

You now know that the way you live your life is in your hands and you have been made extraordinarily capable in the way the unlimited chemistry has brought you about. That is an extraordinary event, an amazing product, and an achievement. And further, this miracle you, developed in a planet created in cosmic explosions which contains all the requirements of your life. It is already here!

Think of that. With atomic particles and forces in far too many possibilities to imagine here you are, and your existence is enviable. You and all of us humans are already a miracle!

What does this mean to you and for you? You are stronger than a wish for something spiritual to rescue you, to take you somewhere safe. You have been formed with a mind of limitless inventiveness. Look at what humankind has created!

Over history, wishing for a spirited overseer to rescue this cosmic reaction us has failed far too many times, for the sick, for the tormented in wars, for the murdered souls from the cruelty of narcissistic leaders who have been unbowed by that prayed for the spirit.

The evidence, the reality has been presented to you.

Q: You are telling me to be grateful for what I have already. You are telling me that the wishing I have been doing is deflecting from reality, that I should use my own abilities, right?

A: Yes, look into yourself and others deeper, stop assuming the problems can be solved by the spiritual outside of you. You exist in Reality!

Q: But my soul, what about my soul, can't I go on?

A: The soul has been termed the God within each of us. And that is what it is. It is the composite of your thoughts and hopes and morality and all within.

Q: Surely there is more, isn't there?

A: Yes, though the pathway is one of a different course than going to some magic place, sins and all hanging all over you.

In fact, the religious beliefs over time, all have in their core, benevolence for other humans. That same foundation is there within all of us.

What this does in effect if practiced is recognize that <u>we are a Species</u>, and our longevity depends upon our caring for the good of all our offspring to come. Work to ensure you are good the best you can be in safety for your grandchildren. They have the genetics of you. Your genetics, your genome [1]will go on if we humans provide for each other into the future.

1.A genome is an organism's **complete set of genetic information**. A genome includes all the hereditary instructions for creating and maintaining life, as well as for instructions for reproduction. The human genome, like all other cellular life forms, consists of DNA and includes both nuclear and mitochondrial DNA. Each genome contains **the information needed to build and maintain that organism throughout its life**. Your genome is the operating manual containing all the instructions that helped you develop from a single cell into the person you are today. There are many ways and resources that a person's genomes can be "Banked."

Your chance to live forever is to maintain your fellow humans to survive on behalf of you to establish the distant future.

In the end, it all has to do with the ability of humankind to mature, to be empathetic to our species, one and all, as a most central aspect of our behavior.

Future us will, if we achieve that, indeed master movement into the cosmos. These later forms of us, we shall call them Homo vistavien will find a home, and there establish Vistavia, a perfect world.

Given the chance to exist their intelligence will be far above us now, indeed much within them will be human memory captured and very probably be in reformatted bodies.

"In this future, we might build enormous space power plants around black holes, lowering masses toward them to harvest their gravitational pull like the weights pulling down in a grandfather's clock, says Princeton physicist J. Richard Gott. Or we might tap the internal heat of planets to generate energy: The gravitational interaction between celestial bodies creates friction, which can keep planets hot inside even without any star-shine."

Thus, "do not picture cave dwellers huddling around geothermal heaters. Trillions of years of evolution will have long since have transformed us," Laughlin says.

That is, in that vast far away time those memory genetics will be reformulated for many now living by your ultra-great grandchildren. These will be moved to a new human form in that Vistavia. "We will have merged with our computers. We will not even have a physical form. But we humans will be there within.

The thing our descendants will have in common with us is the essential spark of life: not flesh and blood necessarily but information. Yes, that wonderful, magic creation-the human being can still be there if we guard its benevolent imprint. That is if we protect the children so our species can go on!

"That's the most important lesson from thinking about the far future universe," Laughlin says. "We are being naïve when we think of life only in terms of Earthlike planets and carbon-based life.

Information-based life can keep going forever. The gravitational era that begins around 15 trillion years from now could continue for quintillion years and beyond, Laughlin estimates. A quintillion is a 1 followed by 18 zeroes. It is trillion times as long as the entire history of our hominid line on Earth."

So, within you is the miracle. You are a part of the whole of it. The remarkable gift is you are human- unique, One that can change, You have the will. It is gifted by cosmic chemistry. You have the brain, and the ability to think to make yourself the best possible.

In short within us is god gained from the cosmos!

R: Old man, I do struggle with this we have shared, that you have presented, but I do see that I have depended too little on myself. I know you have put it all in a written form as you told me earlier. I would love to have a copy of that to share as my time moves on.

A: I will see to that. We will call it "Someone Finds Answers."

AUTHORSHIP

This in its 'book form" as you have it, was compiled from a set of scientific presentations, available on the Internet that was shared between friends. It was restored by editor D.M. Yourtee from the files of Minds-Eye Manuscripts, LLC a company that publishes works focusing on ways to secure the future for Humankind.

The reader will have noted that the contributors of the scientific information reported-diligently documented knowledge of our Universe. The book could not have been accomplished without their insight which is indeed, appreciated.

This is a Future Navigator Book. Following are others in the series. All relate to issues and solutions for securing the future of our children.

Future Navigators Arise (ISBN:978-1-71-407029-9)

A Navigators Journey Through Time (ISBN: 978-0-46-468656-9)

The Omega Shield (ISBN 9878-1-38-989564-7)

Offspring (ISBN: 978-1-38-801961-7) and

The Final Boundary (ISBN 978-0-46-465360-8).

A Note: Invariably books will be published with similar titles (Someone gets Answers, Someone Believes Other Answers, etc.).

This is certainly acceptable, as open discourse is very healthy.

Hope is that such publications do not create bias, hate or prejudice against anyone. We humans are to have a future if we respect each other.

From the Minds-Eye

Grand Junction, CO.

Correspondence to Minds-Eye at Bresnan.net

Sales web site www.aminds-eyejourney.net

Print Store blurb.com/store

Reviews regarding Minds-Eye Manuscripts and Books:

"An engaging search for higher meaning in life, challenging rational thinking about the value and future of Humans."
  Online Review of books and Current Affairs.

"Vital read as we will become increasingly aware of our present journey toward survival or extinction."
  "Mind Quest"

www.ingramcontent.com/pod-product-compliance
Lightning Source LLC
Chambersburg PA
CBHW061709120626
46550CB00003B/1158